She Was My First Love

Love

(The Love That Knows No End)

A Novel by:- Adish

Adish

INTRODUCTION

You can never truly understand the beauty and value of love until your heart falls apart. This book is not just a collection of words; it is a reflection of my journey— of love, heartbreak, and the search for meaning in between .If you've ever felt lost, struggled in relationships, or searched for hope while trying to rediscover yourself, you might find pieces of your own story within these pages.

No matter how difficult life has been, no matter how exhausted you feel, there is always a reason to keep going. Even in the shattered pieces of a broken heart, there is hope—just as a wilted rose may lose its beauty, yet its fragrance lingers. Pain does not erase the possibility of happiness; it only reshapes it.

This book is for those who are trying to heal from the things they cannot put into words. You are not alone in your journey, and healing is always within reach.

Adish

"Even in the silence of a broken heart, love lingers—like a feather carried by the wind, refusing to be lost."

Adish

Preface

A dead rose still smells great !!

Not all love stories end with happily-ever-after, and not all heartbreaks fade away with time. Some memories linger, etched deep within us, like scars we learn to live with. This is one such story, a tale of love so profound, it defied the boundaries of time, and pain so piercing, it became my greatest teacher. A journey through moments that shaped me, broke me, and taught me to grow.

I write not to reopen wounds but to let them heal. This story is not just mine; it belongs to anyone who has loved deeply, lost painfully, and yet found the courage to stand again. To those who feel like their world has crumbled, I want to remind you that even a dead rose retains its fragrance, proof that beauty and meaning can persist even in the face of despair.

There is a part of me that still waits, a stubborn fragment of my heart that refuses to give up. "Come back anytime, even after years," it whispers. "I'll be waiting for you, with the same feeling. No matter how painful it is." These words are both a burden and a source of hope, an anchor that reminds me of the depth of what I once felt.

Adish

She was my first love

I never imagined I would write this, but perhaps it's the only way to find closure. What happened between us remains a mystery even to me, a blend of love, loss, hope, and waiting.

The characters in this narrative are veiled, their identities hidden, not out of shame but out of respect. The emotions, however, are raw and unfiltered, drawn from the deepest corners of my soul.

As you turn these pages, I hope you find a piece of your story in mine. Let this book be a reminder that no matter how dark life gets, there is always light waiting to break through. This is a tale of love, loss, and resilience, a testament to the human spirit's ability to heal, rebuild, and inspire.

The rest, I'll let you discover.

Adish

"Sometimes, love isn't a sudden storm but a quiet realization, growing in the spaces between laughter, distance, and unspoken words."

Adish

Chapter One :- The Start Of A Silent Promise

It all began in 2015. She was just a girl from my neighborhood, someone I casually knew, played with in the streets, unaware that she would one day become the center of my universe. We were friends, simple and carefree, but there was always something about her-the way she laughed, the way she spoke-that caught my attention.

But I was still learning what love was. I didn't fully understand that love needed more than just feelings. It needed attention, communication, and time. I was young, unsure of how to navigate the depth of my emotions.

We were both living our lives, caught up in our own worlds. I, however, couldn't stop thinking about her. She lingered in my thoughts-her smile, her voice, the way she made everything seem a little brighter. But I didn't know how to bridge the gap. Love was new to me, and I wasn't sure how to make her see how much she meant to me.

Adish

She was my first love

"*Some moments change everything—not because they were planned, but because they were meant to be. A few simple words, and life takes a turn you never saw coming.*"

Adish

Then came August 14th, 2018. A date that would mark the beginning of everything. After years of waiting, I finally found the courage to confess. We were both part of the same group, hanging out as friends, but my heart had been beating for her in silence, all along. I remember the moment like it was yesterday. Around 5 pm, everything seemed to slow down. I walked up to her, my pulse racing, my mind spinning with fear and hope. And then, in a moment of clarity, I spoke the words that had been building up inside me for so long.

I like you," I said. Simple. Honest. But heavy with everything I felt.

She looked at me, and for a moment, time stopped. And then, just as quickly, she said the words that changed everything.

"I like you too."

I could hardly believe it. After everything-the waiting, the silence, the uncertainty-she felt the same way. That was the moment the story truly began. But it wasn't easy. It wasn't a fairy tale. We still had to navigate the complexities of our feelings, the growing pains of love, and the weight of what it meant to be in each other's lives

For a whole year after that, we didn't talk much. We were both still finding our way. I didn't know back then that love needed more than just a confession-it needed

Adish

She was my first love

"Sometimes, love doesn't need grand gestures or perfect timing. Sometimes, it just needs a simple message—a quiet spark to remind us that no distance or silence can truly erase what's meant to be."

Adish

attention, communication, and understanding. I was still figuring out what it meant to really love someone. But even in that silence, even in the space between us, my feelings for her never faded. And then, after months of not talking, she texted me. It wasn't a grand gesture, just a simple message asking about someone else. But that one message brought everything back to life. It was like a breath of fresh air after a long, suffocating wait.

We began communicating through texts, sharing thoughts, jokes, and little bits of our lives. But we couldn't meet not yet. Meeting in our own neighborhood felt like an impossible dream. There was a constant awareness of eyes around us, watching, judging. So, we stayed in the realm of messages, of words that bridged the gap between us.

But it was during one of those quiet moments, during a game of truth or dare with friends, that I did something I'd never live down. I dared to do something crazy, and in that moment, I acted on impulse. I cut my hand and wrote the first letter of her name on my skin. It was a foolish, impulsive act, one that I didn't think would have any major consequences

"Some moments in life leave scars—not just on the skin, but on the soul. And yet, even in regret, there's a strange kind of beauty in knowing how deeply we once felt."

Adish

But my family found out. The sight of my bleeding hand sent them into a panic, and the consequences were immediate. My father was furious. The pain from his anger cut deeper than any physical wound. I knew it was a stupid thing to do, but in that moment, it felt like the only way to show her just how deeply I felt. It was cringe, worthy, cheap, and impulsive. Looking back, I can't help but cringe at my younger self. But that was the reality of it, that was the kind of love I thought I was capable of. Foolish, reckless, and pure all at once. Despite the consequences, despite the mistakes, I waited. I waited for her, for us, for something to finally fall into place. And in the end, I realized that waiting was part of the journey, the patience, the longing, the hope that no matter what, love would find a way.

The story of us truly began there with tentative steps, cautious yet filled with hope. Looking back, I see this chapter of my life as the beginning of a silent promise, one that spoke of love, patience, and the courage to keep going, even when the road ahead seemed unclear.

But love has its own way of testing us, often in the most unexpected ways. Our story wasn't one of grand gestures or picture, perfect moments; it was built on quiet conversations, stolen glances, and the kind of bond that words could never fully capture.

Adish

She was my first love

"*Not all love stories begin with grand moments; some start with a single message, a quiet reassurance that distance never truly meant goodbye.*"

Adish

Her first text after months of silence felt like a bridge, closing the gap that had grown between us. We started communicating more, though always cautiously, as if afraid of what the world might think or say. Every text from her felt like a piece of her heart shared with mine, and I cherished each word like a treasure.

Yet, there were challenges both internal and external. I often questioned myself, wondering if I was enough for her, if I could be the person she deserved. At the same time, the watchful eyes of our small community made even the simplest interactions feel like an impossible task. But through it all, there was a quiet determination in me, a belief that what we had was worth every obstacle we faced.

The moments we couldn't meet were filled with dreams of what could be. I imagined us walking together in the open, without fear or hesitation. I dreamed of a day when the world would fade away, and it would just be the two of us, free to love without boundaries. Those dreams kept me going, even when reality felt heavy.

Looking back now, I see that those early days, though imperfect, were the foundation of something beautiful. They taught me patience, resilience, and the importance of holding onto hope, even when the odds seemed stacked against us.

Adish

She was my first love

"*Some bonds don't need constant presence; they survive in unspoken promises, in the quiet certainty that no matter the distance, they still belong.*"

Adish

And so, with every passing day, our silent promise grew stronger, a promise that, no matter what lay ahead, we would find a way to keep our story alive.

Adish

"*Love doesn't follow rules—it finds cracks in the walls built to keep it out, slipping through stolen moments and whispered words, refusing to be silenced.*"

Adish

Chapter Two:- The Cost Of Holding On.

The days after our story began were anything but easy. What started with stolen texts and whispered feelings soon turned into a battle against circumstances I wasn't prepared for. My parents, already aware of her name from the dramatic incident with my hand, were now on high alert. They didn't see the innocence in my actions, only the rebellion of a boy too young to understand love.

At that age, I didn't have my own phone, and after they discovered I was still chatting with her, they made sure I wouldn't get the chance again. My access to any device was restricted, and the few moments I managed to get a hold of a phone were carefully monitored.

But love doesn't understand boundaries. Where there's a will, there's always a way. I became resourceful unlocking phones with tricks I picked up, sneaking moments of connection whenever I could. The stolen conversations, though brief and risky, meant the world to me. Each message, no matter how short, felt like a lifeline, keeping our bond alive.

Despite the challenges, we grew closer. What began as fleeting texts turned into heartfelt exchanges. Each word carried a depth that only young love could possess,

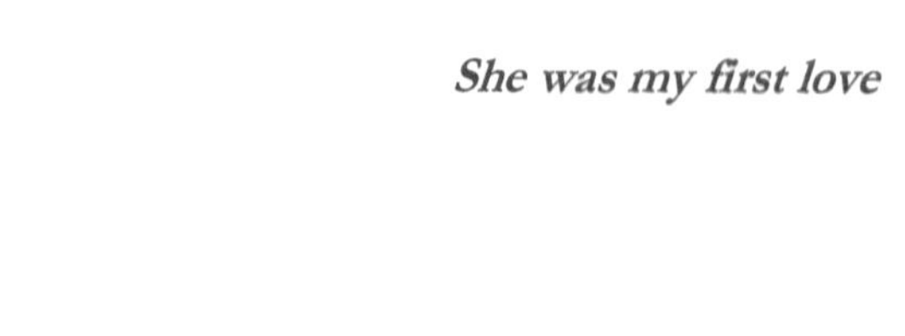

"Some connections defy distance, disapproval, and time. They may bend under pressure, but the memories remain unshaken."

Adish

simple, yet powerful. Eventually, our connection grew beyond words on a screen. Meeting in person was a challenge. In a neighborhood where everyone knew everyone, finding privacy was almost impossible. Yet, we managed. The buildings in our area became our secret meeting spots. They were far from ideal, but they gave us a chance to be close, to share moments that words couldn't capture.

Her mother, in contrast to mine, was more understanding. She was a friend to her daughter, someone she could confide in. I asked her to share our story with her mom, hoping for her support. While her mother didn't oppose our bond outright, she laid down a condition that if the world found out about us, she wouldn't be able to stand up for her daughter. It wasn't approval, but it wasn't rejection either. It was a gray area I wasn't sure how to navigate.

Meanwhile, my parents' disapproval grew stronger. Each time I was caught chatting with her, the consequences became harsher. Phones were locked away, conversations were monitored, and punishments came swiftly. But the love I felt for her was unyielding. I took the beatings, endured the scolding, and unlocked the phones over and over again. No matter the cost, I couldn't let go of what we had.

Still, we tried our best to hold onto what we had, no matter the hurdles. But some moments are destined to test us in ways we can't imagine. One day, on my

She was my first love

"Some moments don't just pass; they stay with you, shaping you into someone you never thought you'd become."

Adish

birthday, a day I hoped would be special for us, we decided to meet. It was supposed to be a simple, happy moment between us. But fate had other plans.

Her uncle saw us that day. What could've been just another secret meeting quickly turned into chaos. He wasted no time informing both her parents and mine about what he had seen. That moment became one of the most dangerous and unforgettable events of my life.

Instead of celebrating, I spent my birthday in tears. What should have been a day of joy became a memory filled with heartbreak. It felt like everything we had worked so hard for was unraveling in front of us. That incident led to a painful gap in our connection. Communication stopped, and the meetings that had once kept us close became impossible.

I vividly remember sitting alone in my room that night, staring at the ceiling, wondering where it all went wrong. My heart ached for her, yet I couldn't reach out. Each moment of silence felt like an eternity. It wasn't just the loss of communication; it was the fear that I might lose her altogether.

Even after the incident, her face never left my mind. Every corner of my room, every quiet moment, every fleeting memory brought her back to me. Love, I realized, wasn't just a feeling it was a longing, a quiet desperation that refused to fade. My heart still beat for her, even when I couldn't reach her. It was the kind of

Adish

She was my first love

"*Some people leave, not because they want to, but because life gives them no other choice. And sometimes, holding on means letting go.*"

Adish

ache only love could cause a beautiful, painful reminder of the connection we had.

In those moments, I realized that love isn't just about the smiles, the stolen glances, or the sweet texts. Love is about endurance, the willingness to hold on even when the world seems set against you. And though the distance between us felt unbearable, I held on to the belief that this was just another storm we had to weather. It was more than just missing someone, it was a test of resilience, the test of keeping a piece of yourself alive for someone who might never be able to return it.

What hurt the most wasn't the scolding or the punishments, it was the silence. The gap that stretched between us felt like an endless void. I wondered if she missed me the way I missed her. Did she think of me when she closed her eyes? Did her heart ache the way mine did?

This wasn't the last time something like this would happen. Our journey was filled with countless battles, both big and small. But that day, on my birthday, I learned a lesson that would stay with me forever: true love is not just about being together; it's about the fight to stay together, even when the odds seem insurmountable. And although I didn't have her in my life at that moment, I knew one thing for sure: I would always carry the lessons of our love with me, no matter where it took me.

Adish

She was my first love

In the end, no matter how much you fight to keep them, people always find a way to leave.

Adish

As time passed, I realized that love, in all its forms, teaches you more than any other experience in life. It's not about how many times you're able to meet, how many texts you send, or the number of moments you share. It's about the choices you make when you're faced with obstacles. Every time we were apart, the longing only made me appreciate the strength of the bond we had more. And even if circumstances kept us apart, the love remained, nestled deep within my heart.

Eventually, I came to understand that sometimes, love isn't meant to flourish in the way you want it to. But that doesn't make it any less significant. The pain, the joy, the trials, and the triumphs all of them were part of a greater story. A story that, even though it was painful at times, shaped me into the person I would become.

The journey wasn't just about love, but about self-discovery. I learned to recognize my own resilience, the quiet strength that I never knew existed within me. The silence that followed her absence became a teacher in itself. In the midst of that silence, I was forced to face my own fears, insecurities, and hopes. Love, in its truest form, wasn't always about being together. It was about growth; personal growth, growth in understanding, and growth in how to let go when necessary.

As I moved forward, I began to understand that letting go didn't mean forgetting. It didn't mean that the memories would fade or that the love would disappear. It meant accepting that sometimes, things are out of

Adish

She was my first love

"Some loves don't fade; they simply transform into the lessons
that guide us forward."

Adish

your control. And despite the heartbreak, the anger, and the tears, you learn to hold on to what you can: the lessons, the moments, and the love that shaped you.

That chapter of my life taught me that love is not a simple, linear journey. It's full of unexpected turns, challenges, and detours. And sometimes, the most painful moments become the most pivotal. They shape who you are, and what you carry with you, even when you think you're leaving it all behind.

What I had with her wasn't just a relationship, it was a chapter that defined my understanding of connection. It made me realize that no matter how much time passed, no matter how many other experiences I had, a part of me would always be tied to her. Not in the way I had once envisioned, but in the deeper, more personal way that comes with a love that is left unspoken, untouched, yet forever imprinted on the soul.

And so, as I moved forward with my life, I carried with me not just the lessons of our love, but a renewed understanding of what it means to hold on and let go, of what it means to love fiercely, even when circumstances seem impossible.

Adish

I make bad decisions, and I don't want you to be one of them. I can't love you—not because I don't want to, but because love has a way of breaking everything it touches. It shatters, it takes, it leaves behind nothing but empty spaces where something beautiful once existed. And when two people who were once in love walk away, they don't just lose each other—they lose everything. I'd rather keep you in any way I can than risk losing you completely.

Adish

Because sometimes, love is not about staying in the same place, but about learning to grow from the spaces you once shared. And in the end, that's the real cost of holding on— the cost of learning to evolve while holding onto the parts of the past that shaped you, while continuing to move forward into a future that is uncertain, but filled with hope.

Adish

She was my first love

"If he truly loves her, he won't be the weight that holds her down, but the wind that helps her rise."

Adish

Chapter Third:- Against The Odds.

As the years passed, what started as a fragile connection grew into a deep and undeniable bond. There were moments we stole from the world, moments that felt like small victories against the odds. Despite all the hurdles, parental restrictions, societal scrutiny, and our own immaturity, our love found ways to flourish.

Summers brought a different kind of freedom. The vacations gave us an excuse to spend more time together. We no longer confined ourselves to sneaky meetings in buildings; we began venturing outside. Each stolen hour felt like a treasure, every conversation a thread weaving us closer together. It was as though the universe conspired to give us those fleeting moments, even as we knew deep down that the peace we found wouldn't last forever.

Day by day, our bond grew stronger. With every laugh, every shared secret, and every silent moment where words weren't necessary, we built a world of our own. It wasn't perfect, but it was ours. I could see her becoming more than just someone I loved. She became my safe place, my reason to smile amidst the chaos.

But just as life seemed to settle into a rhythm of hope and love, the world around us changed in ways we could

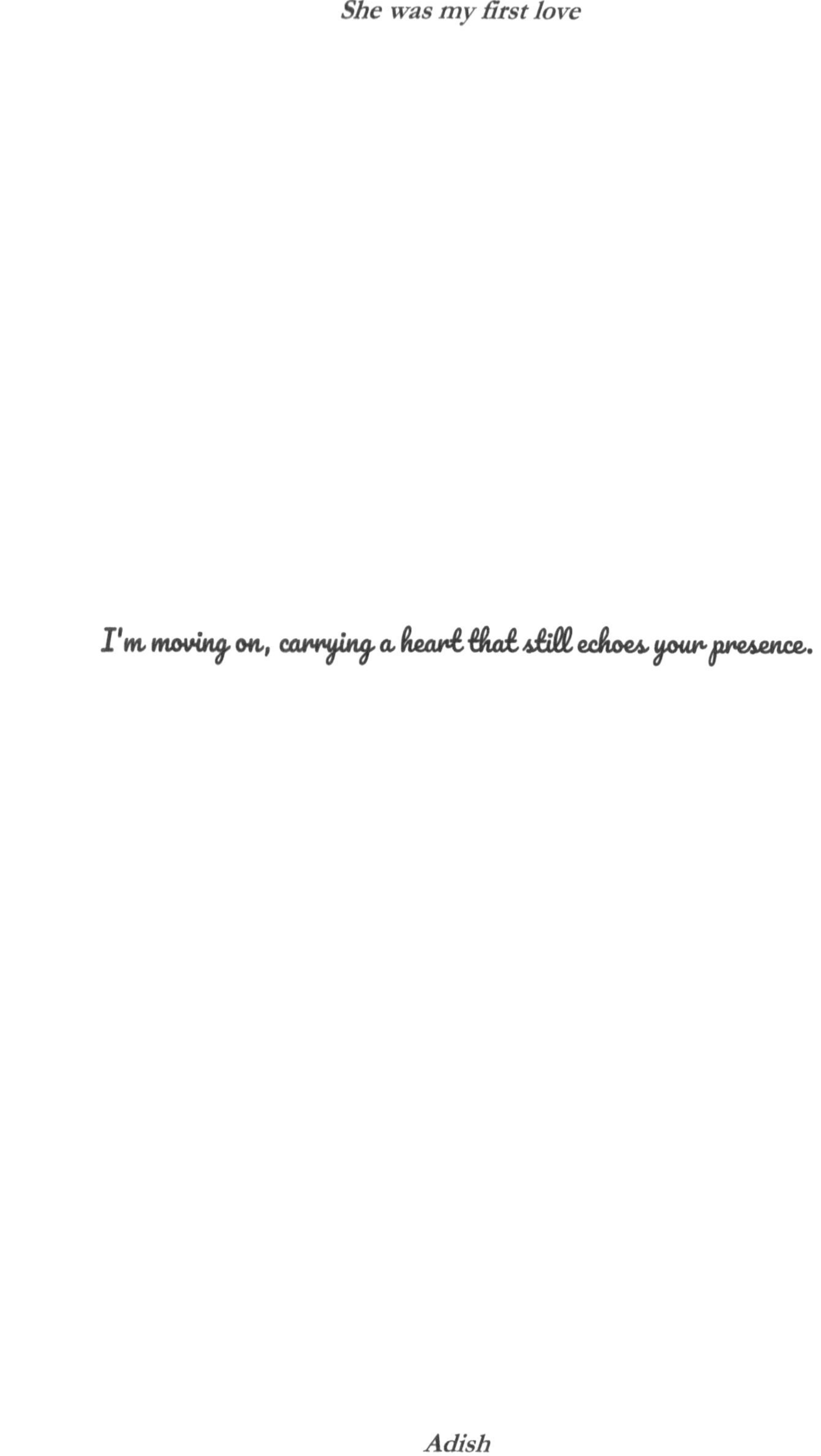
She was my first love

I'm moving on, carrying a heart that still echoes your presence.

Adish

have never imagined. The dark phase of our story began when the virus swept across the globe. What started as whispers of a distant threat soon turned into an undeniable reality. Lockdowns were imposed, and the world came to a standstill.

For us, it felt like the universe was testing our connection once again. Despite living in the same society, the restrictions made meeting impossible. The streets that once felt alive with the rhythm of daily life were eerily silent. What had once been obstacles we could overcome now felt like immovable walls.

The absence of physical presence was unbearable. We could no longer share fleeting touches, stolen glances, or whispered confessions. Our conversations were reduced to text messages and voice calls, but even those lacked the warmth we found in each other's presence.

Yet, even in the midst of this separation, we tried to hold on. I'd sit by the window, staring at the empty streets below, imagining her doing the same. It felt like the distance between us was more than just physical, it was emotional, a cruel reminder of how fragile love can feel in times of uncertainty.

The lockdown taught us the value of patience and resilience. We learned to appreciate the moments we had shared in the past, holding onto them like fragments of light in the darkness. Memories of our summer meetings played like a reel in my mind. I'd think about

Adish

She was my first love

"Love isn't tested in moments of ease; it's forged in the silence, in the waiting, in the quiet battles no one else sees."

Adish

the way her laughter would echo in the empty streets, how her presence could make even the mundane feel extraordinary.

But even as the distance tested us, it also reminded me of the strength of our bond. There were moments of doubt, of course. Moments where the silence felt too loud, where I questioned whether we could weather yet another storm. But every time, the love we had built over the years reminded me to hold on just a little longer.

Lockdown was not just a test of our love; it was a lesson in endurance. It showed me that love isn't just about being together in the easy moments. It's about holding on through the storms, finding ways to stay connected even when the world seems determined to pull you apart.

As the days turned into weeks and the weeks into months, I found myself growing in ways I hadn't expected. The pain of separation taught me to value the little things: the warmth of her voice, the way she said my name, the memories we had created together. It wasn't the same as being with her, but it was enough to keep me going.

The lockdown may have kept us apart physically, but it couldn't erase the connection we had built. If anything, it strengthened our resolve to fight for what we had. The world outside was uncertain, but the love we shared

Adish

We got scared—scared of falling too deep, of losing ourselves in love. In our fear of attachment, rejection, and abandonment, we lost it all. We drowned in thoughts of not being enough or being too much. In trying to protect ourselves, we built walls so high that even love couldn't climb over them.

(We didn't say it; but we felt it.)

Adish

remained a constant, a reminder that even in the darkest times, there is light to be found.

And so, even as the virus loomed over our lives, I held onto the belief that this was just another phase one we would overcome together. Because in the end, love isn't about the moments when everything is perfect. It's about holding on, no matter how hard the world tries to tear you apart.

The story of our bond didn't end with the lockdown. It was just another chapter, another trial that would shape the love we shared. And as I looked toward the uncertain future, I knew one thing for certain: no matter what came next, our love would find a way to endure.

Adish

She was my first love

"Some battles in love aren't fought with words or actions, but with patience—the quiet kind that waits even when the world says to let go."

Adish

Chapter Four:-Trials of Conviction

As the world slowly began to reopen after months of lockdown, it brought with it a new set of challenges for us. Just when it felt like we were finding our rhythm again, life decided to test us once more. My parents, always watchful and skeptical about our bond, discovered about us again. This time, their disapproval was stronger, and it left no room for negotiation. Meeting her became impossible, and even communicating felt like a distant dream.

For weeks, our connection faltered not because we wanted it to, but because the circumstances forced us apart. Yet, love has its ways of defying odds. Every day, I found myself standing outside her class, waiting for a chance to talk to her, to convince her that this wasn't the end. For a month, this became my routine a silent rebellion against the forces trying to keep us apart.

She was hesitant, and understandably so. The weight of expectations, the fear of what lay ahead, and the constant scrutiny from those around us made her question if we could truly endure it all. And just as I was beginning to get through to her, a new voice entered the conversation, her mother.

Adish

She was my first love

If a heart truly wants to stay, it stays. If hands truly wish to hold, they do not let go. If it is love, it comes willingly ,without doubt, without excuses.

Adish

Her mom approached me one day, not with anger but with concern. Her words were calm yet piercing, carrying a tone of pragmatic wisdom:
"In the future, you both will go to college, and life will change. You'll meet new people, have new friend circles, and maybe even find new love. That's just how life is."

Her words stung, not because I believed them but because they came from a place of misunderstanding. She didn't see the bond we shared, the sacrifices we had made, or the depth of our feelings. To her, it was just a phase, something fleeting and replaceable. But I knew better. I knew that what we had wasn't ordinary, and I wasn't going to let someone else's doubts dictate our story.

While I respected her mother's perspective, I focused on convincing the one person who truly mattered to her. For days, I poured my heart into every conversation, every message, every look we exchanged. I reminded her of all we had endured and all we had to look forward to. I assured her that no matter what her mom or my parents said, we would find a way to make this work.

Eventually, she believed me. The trust we had built over the years proved stronger than the doubts down by others. We promised each other that no matter how hard things got, we would stick together. Our bond was worth fighting for, and we weren't going to let anyone else define our future.

Adish

She was my first love

"*Life is not a straight path; it bends, breaks, and often leads us through shadows before guiding us to the light we never knew we needed.*"

(*Everything happens for a reason.*)

Adish

This phase of our journey taught me that love isn't just about the moments of happiness and ease. It's about standing firm in the face of opposition, about proving the depth of your feelings not just to the world but to the one you love. And though the road ahead still held uncertainties, we were ready to face them together.

Our promise to face them together marked a turning point in our relationship. It wasn't just words, it was a commitment to weather every storm, to fight for what we believed was worth holding on to. Life, however, had its way of testing that promise again and again.

As days turned into weeks, the world around us continued to shift. College was on the horizon, and with it came the inevitable question: Would we really be able to keep our bond intact amidst all the new beginnings and distractions? Everyone around us seemed to doubt it, and at times, even we couldn't help but wonder if love alone was enough.

But the beauty of our connection lay in the way we defied expectations. We started finding creative ways to keep our bond alive. Secret notes exchanged through mutual friends, fleeting glances during moments we could steal, and the quiet reassurance that we were still there for each other all of it became the foundation of a new chapter in our relationship.

Her mother's words, though hurtful, lingered in the back of my mind. "New love," she had said, as if love were

Adish

She was my first love

"*Maybe the heart never truly unlearns love, but with time, we learn to live with its absence, accepting what can never be ours.*"

Adish

something disposable, something you could simply replace. But each time I thought about those words, they only strengthened my resolve. I didn't want new love. I wanted her. And I wanted to prove to the world and to ourselves that what we had wasn't just a fleeting phase.

There were days when it felt impossible, when the distance, the doubts, and the disapproval of those around us threatened to pull us apart. But every time we came close to breaking, we found a way to remind each other of why we started this journey in the first place.

One moment stands out a night when we were both overwhelmed by the weight of everything happening around us.

It was moments like that which defined our love not the easy times, but the hard ones. The moments when giving up seemed like the simpler choice, but we chose to fight instead.

Slowly, we began rebuilding the little routines that had been taken from us. The whispered promises of a future together became the glue that held us close. And with each passing day, we grew stronger not just as a couple, but as individuals who believed in the power of what we shared.

This chapter of our lives wasn't about grand gestures or dramatic declarations of love. It was about the quiet, everyday acts of defiance that kept our bond alive. It

Adish

She was my first love

Unless you recognize what is unhealthy for you, you can't truly choose what is good for you. Life is about experiencing, learning, and growing. Without risks, there is no wisdom—only the illusion of safety.

Adish

was about proving, to ourselves and to the world, that love isn't just a feeling it's a choice. And we chose each other, again and again, no matter how hard it got.

As I look back on that time, I realize it wasn't just a test of our love, it was a test of our character. It taught us resilience, patience, and the value of fighting for something you truly believe in. And though the road ahead was still uncertain, one thing was clear: as long as we had each other, we could face whatever came our way. Together.

Adish

She was my first love

"You made me believe in something that never existed.
Love was a lie, and the lie was love."

Adish

Chapter Five:- Shattered Connections

After everything we had faced together, I never thought the silence between us could grow deeper, yet it did. Our communication and meetings came to an abrupt halt once more. I couldn't bear the emptiness, the growing distance, or the overwhelming helplessness that came with it. Desperate to bridge the gap, I decided to take a chance and visit her floor, hoping to find a way to reconnect.

I approached her best friend, pleading with her to call her for just a moment. But instead of understanding or lending a hand, her friend did the unthinkable: she called her father and told him about my presence. What followed was a chain reaction that would leave me reeling. Her friend's father wasted no time informing my parents, recounting every detail of the incident.

When the news reached home, it felt like the walls were closing in on me. My parents, already upset about the situation, decided to take even stricter measures. They felt the need to act decisively, believing it was for my own good. The actions they took were firm and left a significant impact on my life, making it clear that they wouldn't tolerate anything that could disrupt their expectations for my future.

She was my first love

"Sometimes the heart shatters in silence, so gently that we don't realize we're bleeding until much later."

Adish

One of the hardest consequences was losing my phone, the last remaining link to her and the imposition of tighter restrictions. My every move was closely watched, leaving me with no way to communicate or reach out to her.

It wasn't just the loss of a device; it was the severing of a connection that had kept me grounded. The absence of her voice, her laughter, and the solace I found in her words created a void I couldn't fill. Each day felt heavier, and the silence between us grew louder with every passing moment.

Despite everything, my feelings for her remained unshaken. Even in the darkest moments, I clung to the memories of our time together. I remembered her smile, the way she looked at me when she was happy, and the promises we had made to face every challenge, no matter how big, side by side.

This chapter of our story was one of the hardest to endure. It tested my patience, my resilience, and my commitment to what we had. The restrictions, the misunderstandings, and the judgments felt like endless hurdles. Yet, amidst the heartbreak and frustration, one thing remained clear I Love isn't just about the moments of joy and connection. It's about holding on when everything around you threatens to tear you apart.

Adish

How blessed I am to understand love, yet how cursed I am to never be the one it chooses.

Adish

Though I didn't know what the future held, I refused to give up on her, on us. I believed that the love we shared was strong enough to endure even the harshest storms. And while I sat in silence, unable to reach her, I held onto the hope that this was just another phase a difficult one, but not the end of our story.

Though the days felt endless and heavy, my heart refused to let go of her. Even without communication, I found myself wondering if she felt the same ache I did. Did she miss me the way I missed her? Did she replay the moments we shared, just as I did every night? These thoughts became both my solace and my torment, a constant reminder of what we had lost and what I was determined to regain.

I began to search for new ways to keep our bond alive, even if only in spirit. I would pass by places we had once visited, imagining her presence beside me. I would glance at her building from afar, wondering if she was looking out at the same time, thinking of me. It was these small acts of hope that kept me going, even when everything felt like it was falling apart.

At home, my parents' strictness didn't waver. Every step I took was under their watchful eyes. Yet, amidst their sternness, I realized something while they didn't understand my love, their actions came from a place of concern. They believed they were protecting me, shielding me from what they saw as a distraction or

Adish

She was my first love

"Why did fate allow our paths to cross at all, if we were strangers before and we are strangers now ?"

Adish

harm. It didn't make their actions any easier to bear, but it gave me a new perspective.

I began to reflect on the depth of my feelings and the strength of the connection we shared. This wasn't just a fleeting emotion or a youthful infatuation. It was something deeper, something that had weathered countless storms and still stood firm. Despite the pain and the challenges, I found myself more certain than ever about what I felt for her.

Days turned into weeks, and weeks into months, but the fire within me didn't fade. I resolved that no matter how long this phase lasted, I would find a way to reconnect with her. I didn't have the answers, and I didn't know how it would happen, but I believed in the strength of our bond.

In those quiet moments of longing, I realized something profound love isn't just about being with someone; it's about carrying them in your heart when they're not there. It's about the unwavering belief that no matter how far apart you are, your connection remains unbroken.

Adish

No matter how heavy life feels, no matter how exhausted you are, there is always a reason to keep going. Even in the ruins of a broken heart, hope lingers—just as the scent of a wilted rose remains long after its petals have faded. Beauty exists even in what seems lost. So never give up—on life, on happiness, or on yourself.

Adish

This phase of our journey was painful and uncertain, but it taught me resilience. It taught me to hold onto hope even when the world seemed intent on pulling us apart. And while I didn't know when or how our paths would cross again, I was certain of one thing this wasn't the end. It was just another chapter in our story, and I was determined to write the next one with her.

Adish

She was my first love

I was the love no one dared to fight for,
I was the love that was never became your priority

Adish

Chapter Six:- Letters Across the Distance

After everything that had unfolded, I found myself in an impossible situation. My parents, in their protective instincts, had banned me from using a phone or any means of communication. They weren't my enemies, they were only doing what they believed was best for me, trying to secure my future and shield me from potential distractions. But no one, not even they, could truly understand the depth of what I felt for her.

I couldn't approach her, couldn't text her, couldn't see her, yet my feelings refused to be silenced. It was in this helplessness that I found a new way, a quiet, patient way to stay connected with her. I began writing letters for her.

Every night, I poured my heart onto the pages of my notebook. I wrote about my day, about how I was handling the situation, and most importantly, about how much I missed her. It became my lifeline, a way to express everything I couldn't say aloud. Each letter was a small piece of my soul, a testament to the love that refused to fade despite the distance and restrictions.

But writing the letters wasn't enough. I needed to get them to her. That's when my friends stepped in. Despite feeling shy and even embarrassed at times, I asked

She was my first love

Nothing shines as brightly,

As you do in my eyes

Adish

them for help. Some of them were younger than me, but they didn't hesitate. They understood what I was going through and supported me in ways I'll never forget.

I'd hand them the letters, carefully folded and tucked into my notebook, and they would pass them along. Sometimes, they'd take photos of the letters and send them to her. Other times, they'd deliver them in person. It wasn't ideal, and it wasn't easy, but it was the only way I could keep her in my life.

She, too, found ways to respond. My friends would lend me their phones, allowing me to read the messages she sent back. It was a delicate system, one that required patience, trust, and an incredible amount of courage from everyone involved. Each message I received from her felt like a victory, a reminder that our connection was still alive, no matter how difficult the circumstances.

But this wasn't enough for me. I craved to see her, to talk to her face-to-face. So, I came up with another plan. I told my parents that I was going out to play with my friends, but in reality, I was borrowing their phones to text her. I would text her, asking if we could meet, begging for just a few stolen moments together.

At first, it was difficult. She was hesitant, knowing the risks we were taking. But eventually, she agreed. There was a place nearby where we could meet in secret a quiet spot, hidden from prying eyes. I would text her

Love doesn't break hearts, people do. I hope you find someone whose touch feels like home and whose presence mends what was once broken.

Adish

from my friend's phone, telling her where and when to come. Then I'd wait, my heart pounding, hoping she would show up.

And she always did.

The moments we shared during those meetings were brief but unforgettable. I still remember the way her face lit up when she saw me, the way her voice softened when we spoke. We didn't have much time, but those fleeting minutes were worth every risk, every lie I had to tell.

As time went on, these secret meetings became more frequent. I became skilled at sneaking away, at convincing my parents that I was just another boy playing with his friends. But in truth, I wasn't playing at all, I was fighting for the person I loved.

These moments taught me the lengths I was willing to go for her. They showed me that love isn't just about grand gestures or perfect timing. It's about the little things—the stolen conversations, the hidden smiles, the quiet determination to be together no matter what.

Looking back, I realize how much courage it took for both of us to keep going. Her willingness to meet me, even when it wasn't easy, spoke volumes about how much she cared. And my determination to find ways to reach her, no matter how impossible it seemed, showed me just how strong love can be.

Adish

She was my first love

Letting go isn't a sign of indifference; sometimes, it's the deepest proof that you cared more than anyone else ever did.

Adish

This chapter of our story was one of resilience and resourcefulness. It wasn't just about surviving the challenges we faced—it was about finding ways to thrive despite them. And though it was one of the most difficult times in our journey, it was also one of the most meaningful. It reminded me that love isn't just about being together; it's about doing whatever it takes to stay together, even when the odds are stacked against you.

She was my anchor, my reason to keep going. No matter how difficult things became, I knew that giving up wasn't an option. Our love was worth fighting for, and I was determined to do whatever it took to keep it alive.

As time went on, the secret meetings became a mix of excitement and fear. Every moment with her felt like a fleeting dream, and the constant worry of getting caught was like a shadow looming over us. Yet, those moments were worth every risk.

We'd talk about everything and nothing, pouring our hearts out during those brief encounters. The world outside seemed to vanish when we were together. The stolen smiles, the quiet laughs, and the gentle touch of her hand were enough to remind me why all this effort was worth it. Each meeting felt like rediscovering our bond, a reassurance that what we had could withstand even the most challenging storms.

Adish

You handed me every reason to leave, yet my stubborn heart still refuses to let go.

Adish

On days we couldn't meet, I'd sit alone and think about her. I'd imagine the sound of her voice, the way her eyes lit up with excitement, and the way she brought a sense of calm into my chaotic world. These memories became my refuge, keeping me afloat in the moments when reality felt unbearable. The thought of her gave me hope, a silent promise that everything would eventually work out.

One day, I realized that words held a power greater than I had ever imagined. With my phone taken away and every other method of communication stripped from me, I turned to writing letters. These weren't just notes—they were pieces of my soul, captured in ink and paper. Every letter I wrote felt like a lifeline, a way to keep our connection alive despite the circumstances. I'd pour my thoughts into a notebook, detailing everything from mundane daily occurrences to the deepest corners of my heart.

Sometimes, I'd slip in a poem, raw and unpolished, but filled with the emotions I couldn't convey otherwise. These poems became my way of telling her how much she meant to me, how her presence was the light that guided me through my darkest days. And through the kindness of a few trusted friends, these letters and poems would reach her. They became our secret language, a thread that tied us together when everything else seemed to pull us apart.

Adish

It's okay to let go when holding on only brings you pain. It's okay to walk away when you've given your all, yet nothing ever changes.

Adish

The role my friends played during this time was something I would always cherish. They didn't just lend me their phones; they lent me their trust, their patience, and their support. They became my bridge to her, carrying my words when I couldn't speak them myself. Whether it was passing a letter or creating excuses to help me sneak out for a few moments, their efforts were a testament to the strength of true friendship.

Yet, this wasn't easy. There were times when the weight of it all felt too heavy to bear. The fear of being caught, the guilt of involving my friends, and the endless battle against circumstances drained me. But even in those moments, the thought of her was enough to keep me going. She was my anchor, my constant in a world that seemed determined to keep us apart.

As the days turned into weeks, I found strength in our resilience. Every small victory a letter delivered, a stolen moment together felt like a triumph. Each of these moments reminded me that love isn't about grand gestures or perfect circumstances; it's about holding on through the storms, finding light even in the darkest corners.

Looking back, it was incredible to see how far we had come. From carefree days filled with laughter to navigating the complexities of secrecy and struggle, our journey was a testament to the power of connection. The challenges we faced didn't weaken our bond; they

Adish

She was my first love

Don't meet my eyes with love if your heart doesn't hold it.
You may pretend, but I will believe—and fall for a beautiful
lie.

Adish

strengthened it, proving that love, in its truest form, could endure anything.

And so, this chapter became more than just a phase of letters and secret meetings; it was a story of patience, perseverance, and the lengths one would go to for the person they love. It was about finding hope in the smallest moments, cherishing the quiet victories, and believing that no matter how impossible the situation seemed, love would always find a way.

She was my first love

It's not about avoiding effort; it's about knowing where to let go. Some things remain beyond our control, no matter how much we give.

Adish

Chapter Seven:- When Time Stood Still

Looking back now, I realize that those months were some of the happiest times of my life. After everything we had endured—the stolen moments, the struggle to stay connected, and the constant fear of losing each other—we finally had something that felt close to normal. It was a time when we weren't just fighting to be together; we were actually living it.

After our 10th grade, we both joined the same computer classes. At first, it felt like a coincidence, but deep down, I knew it was fate giving us another chance. This was our opportunity to be around each other, to share time without sneaking around or relying on others to communicate. And we made the most of it.

Every day, we would reach the classes early, long before they actually started. Those moments before anyone else arrived were ours. She always met me before joining her friends, and in those few minutes, it felt like nothing else in the world mattered. It wasn't about words or grand gestures—it was just about being there, together.

Our favorite part of the day soon became our walks. We never planned them, they just happened naturally. Walking side by side, matching our steps without even

She was my first love

Don't give me that "you're my everything" look. Don't tell me you want me if your only intention is to let me go.

Adish

realizing it, getting lost in conversations that didn't need a destination. We'd talk about everything and nothing, and sometimes, we didn't talk at all—just feeling each other's presence was enough. The world around us blurred into the background, and in those moments, I wished time would stop.

I still remember the way she would tilt her head slightly when she listened, how she'd occasionally glance up at me with that soft expression that made my heart race. The way the afternoon sun caught in her hair as we walked, the way she'd brush a strand behind her ear absentmindedly—it's funny how such small details became the most unforgettable memories.

When class finally started, we'd take our seats, but our conversation never really stopped. It continued in whispers, in glances, in quick messages typed into our phones and erased just as fast. There was a thrill in those stolen exchanges, a silent rebellion against the world that always seemed to find ways to keep us apart.

Three months passed like this—three months of routine, of familiarity, of feeling like we had found a rhythm amidst the chaos of our lives. After class, I always left first, and she followed later with her friends. It was something we never questioned, a small act of caution, though we never imagined we'd need it.

But looking back now, I wish I had held on to those moments a little tighter. Because just when everything

Adish

She was my first love

Sometimes, it takes a goodbye to realize how much you

-cared

Adish

felt safe, when I had started to believe that maybe this time things would be different, life had other plans.

The shift was subtle at first—little things that didn't seem important until they formed a pattern. A sudden tension in her voice when we spoke, messages that took longer to arrive, the way her eyes carried an uncertainty she never voiced. I ignored it, convincing myself it was nothing. Maybe she was just tired, maybe it was something unrelated. But deep down, a small part of me knew— something was changing.

Then, the day came when she told me. The words felt distant, like they didn't belong in our story, yet here they were, forcing their way between us. A decision had been made—one that neither of us had control over. Distance was coming, and there was nothing we could do to stop it.

The world that had felt so stable, so full of possibility, suddenly cracked beneath my feet. All I could do was stand there, trying to make sense of it. Trying to grasp how something that felt so right could still be taken away from us.

The days that followed were filled with an unbearable silence. I kept going to class, hoping for some miracle, for something to change, for her to tell me that there was still a way. But I could see it in her eyes—the hesitation, the helplessness, the unspoken apology. We still had our walks, our moments before class, but they

Adish

She was my first love

If you ever need to walk away from me, I hope it's only to find your way back—with love even stronger than before.

Adish

were different now. The laughter was quieter, the conversations shorter, and every step felt like we were walking toward an inevitable goodbye.

One evening, after class, I stood at the usual spot, watching her leave with her friends. I wanted to call out to her, to ask her to stay just a little longer, but the words never left my lips. I knew she would turn back at least once—she always did. And she did, just before disappearing around the corner. Our eyes met for a fleeting second, and in that moment, I saw everything we couldn't say.

There are some goodbyes that happen slowly, not in a single moment but over days and weeks, in the small spaces between conversations, in the pauses that grow longer, in the messages that stop coming. And sometimes, the worst part isn't the goodbye itself—it's the knowing that it's coming and being powerless to stop it.

I didn't know what lay ahead, but as I walked home that evening, one thought kept repeating in my mind: If I could turn back time, I would have held on tighter. I would have made those three months last a lifetime.

Adish

She was my first love

The deeper we care, the heavier the loss. I've felt your absence with the same intensity that I once fell in love with you.

Adish

Chapter Eight:- Echos of us

Life has a strange way of preparing us for the things we're not ready for. Sometimes, it gives us signs—small moments of change that we brush off, believing everything will remain the same. But in the end, no matter how much we hold on, life moves forward, with or without our permission.

At first, nothing seemed out of the ordinary. We still met, still talked, still walked together like we always did. But beneath those moments of laughter and stolen glances, there was an undercurrent of something unspoken, a weight that neither of us dared to address. She smiled like she always had, but there was something different in her eyes—a hesitation, a lingering sadness she was trying to hide.

I didn't ask. Maybe I should have. Maybe, deep down, I already knew.

One evening, as we sat on the steps outside our class, she held her bag tightly, her fingers gripping the straps as if they were the only thing keeping her grounded. I watched her, waiting for her to say something, but she just let out a soft sigh and looked away.
And then, as casually as if she were telling me about the weather, she said, "My family is moving."

The words barely registered at first. It felt like she had spoken in a language I didn't understand. Moving?

Adish

She was my first love

Take me back to the time when my heart was untouched by pain, when I didn't know what it meant to ache. When I believed that no matter where life led us, what we had would always remain the same. When forever felt real, and I never doubted you. Take me back to the days when we didn't have to pretend to be strangers—when we weren't just you and me, but something more. When we were us.

Adish

Where? When? Why hadn't she told me earlier? A thousand questions rushed to my mind, but I couldn't get a single one out.

I forced a small smile, trying to play it cool, pretending like my heart hadn't just dropped to the pit of my stomach. "Where?"

"Another town. A few hours from here."

A few hours. It didn't sound like much. But in reality, it was a world away.

"When?" I finally managed to ask, my voice quieter than I intended.

"In two weeks."

Two weeks. Fourteen days. That's all we had left.

I wanted to ask why she hadn't told me sooner, why she had kept this from me. But looking at her, I understood. She had been struggling with this just as much as I was. Maybe she hadn't wanted to accept it herself. Maybe she had been waiting for the right moment. Or maybe, just like me, she wasn't ready to let go.

She was my first love

Do they love you for who you are, or do they love the care, time, efforts, and respect you give them?

Adish

That night, I couldn't sleep. My mind kept replaying every moment we had shared, every conversation, every glance, every touch. It felt unfair. After everything we had been through, after all the risks we had taken just to be together, this was how it was going to end? Not because of a fight, not because we wanted to walk away, but because life had decided for us?

For the next few days, I tried to pretend like nothing had changed. We still met, still walked together, still talked about everything and nothing. But there was a shadow looming over us now, a countdown we couldn't ignore.

Each moment felt heavier, more meaningful, like we were trying to memorize every detail, every expression, every second before it slipped away.

The day before she left, we met at our usual spot. The air between us was thick with unspoken words, emotions we didn't know how to express. She looked at me, her eyes searching mine, as if she were trying to remember my face, as if she were trying to capture this moment and keep it with her forever.

"I don't want this to change anything," she said softly.

I wanted to believe her. I wanted to tell her that nothing would change, that we would find a way to make it work. But deep down, I knew the truth. Distance changes everything, no matter how much we fight against it.

Adish

She was my first love

Even when you resist the path ahead, you must walk it—
because this is exactly what life has chosen for you.

Adish

Still, I nodded. "Me neither."

We stood there, the world around us fading into the background. And then, just like that, she turned to leave. I watched her go, my heart screaming at me to stop her, to say something, to do anything. But I didn't.

Some goodbyes don't need words.

The next day, she was gone.

The streets we used to walk felt emptier. The places we had shared felt different, as if they no longer belonged to me alone. I found myself reaching for my phone, wanting to text her, to call her, to hear her voice—just to make sure she was still there, still real.

She texted, of course. At first, every day. Then every other day. And slowly, the gaps between our conversations grew wider. Not because we didn't care, not because we wanted to drift apart, but because life had begun to move forward, pulling us along with it.

But no matter how far she was, no matter how much time passed, one thing remained the same—she was still in my heart.

Distance may have taken her away from me physically, but it could never take her away from where it truly mattered.

Adish

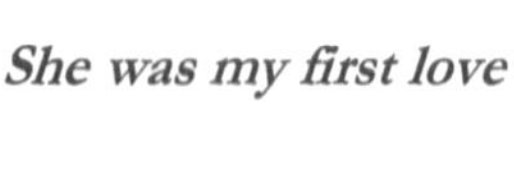

if there's love, there's nothing better than what you've got.

Adish

Chapter Nine:- Distances Measured in Miles

As she left, it felt like a part of my world vanished in an instant. No more sudden meetings, no familiar glimpses of her around the neighborhood—just an emptiness that settled in before I could even process it. It was strange, really. One day, she was there, part of my everyday life, woven into the smallest moments, and the next, she was gone. But deep down, I knew that something had changed. And maybe that's just how life works—we all, at some point, feel the loss of our favorite person, whether it's because they are far away or because something between us has broken.

For the first few days, I didn't know how to react. I told myself it wasn't a big deal; after all, we were still in touch. We still talked, still messaged, still shared our thoughts like we always did. The usual comfort of knowing she was just a street away, that we could meet even if only for a few fleeting minutes, was suddenly ripped away. No more stolen glances, no more unexpected encounters.

But life doesn't wait for you to adjust. As I was still coming to terms with her absence, I made my own decision—to move out of town for my defense studies. It

Adish

She was my first love

"Sometimes, life doesn't ask for our permission to change.
It just moves forward, taking people and places with it, leaving
us to learn how to adapt."

Adish

was a step I had been preparing for, a journey that would define my future, but now, it felt like I was running toward something unknown, leaving behind whatever was left of us.

Moving away wasn't just a shift in location—it was a shift in my entire way of living. At an age when most were still figuring out life within the comfort of their homes, I was thrown into the deep end of independence. From cooking my own meals to washing clothes, from dealing with the monotony of mess food to managing long hours of study, I had no choice but to adapt.

The days were structured, filled with intense training sessions and endless classes. There wasn't much time to breathe, let alone dwell on emotions. But at night, when the world around me quieted, she occupied my thoughts more than ever. I would check my phone, hoping for a message, a call—anything that would remind me that despite the distance, we were still connected.

We talked, but it wasn't the same. The easy conversations we once had now felt measured. The excitement in her messages seemed to dull, as if we were slowly becoming strangers who were just holding onto the habit of talking. I tried to ignore it, brushing it off as a result of our busy schedules, but deep down, a nagging feeling grew inside me.

Protect your energy,
Invest it where it truly matters, Even
the kindest heart, without limits, will
eventually fade.

It started with small things. Messages that once came instantly now took hours. Replies felt shorter, less engaged. I told myself I was overthinking it, that she was adjusting to her new environment just as I was. But overthinking has a way of digging into your mind, making you notice things you'd rather ignore.

Was she losing interest in me? Was I just imagining things, or was something really changing between us? These questions became a constant hum in my mind, affecting me in ways I didn't expect. I became more possessive, more anxious about our conversations. I would find myself rereading old messages, comparing them to the new ones, looking for signs of a shift, of something slipping away.

My insecurities, which I had never truly acknowledged before, surfaced in full force. I started questioning everything—if I was good enough for her, if the distance was too much, if I was doing something wrong. And the more I doubted, the more my emotions took control.

Misunderstandings began to pile up. I found myself overreacting to things I wouldn't have even noticed before. A delayed reply felt like a deliberate act of avoidance. A missed call felt like a sign that I was no longer her priority. I hated that I felt this way, but I couldn't stop it.

Balancing my emotions with the demands of my studies became a challenge I wasn't prepared for. I would sit in

She was my first love

The path life lays before you may not always be easy to walk,
but you must keep moving—because forward is the only way.

Adish

class, staring at my notes but thinking about her. I would try to focus on training, but my mind would drift back to our last conversation, analyzing every word, every pause, every unspoken thought.

I was changing, evolving into someone stronger, more independent. I was learning discipline, resilience, the ability to stand on my own. But was she changing too? And if she was, were we still meant to grow together? Or were we unknowingly growing apart?

The distance between us was no longer just physical—it was something deeper, something I couldn't quite grasp but felt with every passing day. And the hardest part?
Not knowing if I was the only one feeling it.

She was my first love

"I always knew you would break my heart, yet I still chose to love you."

Adish

Chapter Ten: – The End of a Teen Love

This wasn't the end of love, but it was the end of *teen love*—the kind that burns fast and bright, only to be tested by time, distance, and the inevitable realities of life.

Like so many others before us, we faced misunderstandings and the challenges of being apart. But in the end, it wasn't just distance that separated us—it was something stronger, something we had no control over. One day, her mother found our texts. And just like that, everything changed.

She was told to block me, to cut off all contact. It wasn't a choice for her; it was a decision made for her. And while she obeyed, I wasn't ready to let go. She had come into my life like a sudden wave, overwhelming, consuming, and then—just like that—she was gone.

At the same time, life threw another test at me. I lost my grandfather. It felt like everything was falling apart at once. My dreams, my plans, everything I had been holding onto so tightly—it all started slipping through my fingers.

Despite everything, I made a decision. I took a U-turn from that town. I wasn't ready for the solitude, for the emptiness that came with losing her and losing a loved

She was my first love

What is meant for you will never be lost, and what is truly yours will always find its way to you.

Adish

one at the same time. And with my 12th-grade college set to start the next month, along with my defense exams, coming back to my hometown seemed like the only option.

But sometimes, even when we feel like we have to move forward, life has different plans—ones we never saw coming.

But even then, I couldn't move on. I refused to. I couldn't accept that something so important to me could just end like that. So I tried to find a way back to her.

With my 11th-grade final semester ongoing, I used every possible way to reach her. I contacted her friends, convinced them to help me meet her, even if it was just for a moment. From the train station to her college, I followed the paths she walked, hoping for a chance to talk to her.

But every time I managed to reach her, she blocked me again. It was a desperate, painful cycle—me begging for love, and her shutting the door on it. It was no longer the same love that once felt effortless. It had become something one-sided, something that hurt more than it healed.

And that's when I realized—maybe she was right. Maybe listening to her mother, letting go, and moving forward was the best thing for both of us. Even if we wanted to be together, life had already decided otherwise.

Adish

She was my first love

This was my story. But in some way, it's everyone's story. We all have our first love, our first school or college crush. We've all made those silly attempts to impress someone, believing that love could last forever.

But sometimes, fate has its own plans. And no matter how hard we try to hold on, some people are only meant to be a chapter in our story—not the whole book.

Adish

She was my first love

*"Some people come into our lives like passing seasons–never meant
to stay, but always meant to change us."*

Adish

"Writing this book was like reliving moments that
shaped me, moments that made me understand
love, loss, and the power of moving forward. If you've
ever felt something similar, know that
you're not alone. Every love story, whether it
lasts a lifetime or just a chapter, leaves behind a
lesson. Thank you for being part of this journey."

Adish

The End